# Desserts you Deserve!

Mouth Watering Mediterranean Dessert Recipes – to Recreate at Home!

BY

**Christina Tosch**

# Copyright Notes

# Table of Contents

# Introduction

From Italian Affogato to Zuppe Inglese, Mediterranean desserts are the best. What's more, you don't need to be a pastry chef to recreate them at home.

Yogurt from Greece, dried apricots from Turkey, pistachios from Morocco, raisins from Egypt, and soft Italian cheeses are just some of the great-tasting ingredients that go into making mouth-watering Mediterranean desserts.

From easy to make sweet treats to sensational showstoppers, spoil yourself, your family, and your friends to the Mediterranean dessert you all deserve.

Warm, chilled, sweet, or tart all of these Mediterranean desserts are so delicious that everyone will be begging you for the recipe!

Whether you love Greek baklava, Turkish Delight, French Madeleine's, Croatian plum dumplings, or Tunisian almond balls, you will discover precisely what you're looking for right here!

So, when those sweet cravings get a hold, let go of the guilt and choose from these 40 mouth-watering Mediterranean Dessert Recipes.

# Affogato

The secret to the success of this fun Italian dessert rests in the quality of the ice cream you use combined with the intensity of the coffee.

**Servings:** 2

**Total Time:** 5mins

**Ingredients:**

- 2 shots of hot espresso
- 4 scoops of vanilla ice cream
- ½ ounce hazelnut liqueur

**Directions:**

1. Brew the espresso.
2. Add 2 scoops of ice cream to 2 glass dessert bowls.
3. Pour the espresso over the ice cream followed by the hazelnut liqueur.
4. Serve and enjoy.

# Albanian Tespixhe

This rich and sugary cake is almost like a biscuit. It has a soft texture, and in Albanian homes, they often serve it at special events.

**Servings:** 12

**Total Time:** 2hours 30mins

**Ingredients:**

- 1 cup milk
- 5 ounces cup olive oil
- 3 tbsp sugar
- 1 tsp baking soda
- 10½ ounces flour

**Sugar Water:**

- 7¾ ounces sugar
- 1¾ cups water

**Directions:**

1. For the dough: Over moderate heat, mix the milk with the olive oil, sugar, and baking soda. Once the mixture begins bubbling, remove the pan from the pan and add the flour, mixing to create a soft dough.
2. Lightly grease a 12" round baking pan with oil.
3. Roll the dough around the baking pan to make a smooth texture. Press the dough into the bottom and edges of the pan to an even thickness of ⅓".
4. Using a fork, make dot patterns into the dough.
5. Bake in the oven at 355 degrees F for approximately 25 minutes.
6. To make the sugar water: In a small pan, combine the sugar with the water over moderate heat. Once boiling and the water entirely dissolves, remove the pan from the heat and allow to cool.
7. Remove the Tespixhe from the oven.
8. Pour the sugared water over the Tespixhe to entirely cover, and approximately ⅓" up the baking pan to soak into the baked dough while cooling.
9. Once the dessert is cool, transfer to the fridge for a minimum of 60 minutes before slicing and serving.

# Algerian Lemon and Olive Oil Cookies

These ring-shaped cookies flavored with lemon and vanilla are crisp, crumbly, and baked to golden perfection.

**Servings:** 30

**Total Time:** 55mins

**Ingredients:**

- 3 large eggs
- 1 cup granulated sugar
- ½ cup olive oil
- 1 tbsp lemon zest
- 1½ tsp vanilla essence
- 2½ cups unbleached all-purpose flour
- 1 tsp baking powder
- Pinch of salt

**Topping:**

- 1 egg
- ½ tbsp orange blossom water
- Granulated sugar (for sprinkling)

**Directions:**

1. Preheat the main oven to 350 degrees F. Using parchment paper line 2 baking sheets.

2. In a stand mixer with a paddle, beat the eggs with the sugar until pale and light. Gradually and slowly beat in the oil, followed by the lemon zest and vanilla essence.

3. In a second bowl, whisk the flour with the baking powder and salt. Mix into the egg-sugar until just combined.

4. Scoop out 1 tablespoonful of dough and using damp hands, roll into balls and arrange on the baking sheet. The balls should be 2" apart from one another. Repeat the process until all of the balls are made.

5. Make an indent in the middle of each ball to create a ½" impression.

6. In a small-size bowl, beat the egg together with the orange water and brush the mixture lightly over the cookies.

7. Sprinkle sugar over the cookies and bake in the oven for 15-18 minutes, or until golden.

8. Transfer the cookies to a wire baking rack and allow to cool.

9. Repeat the process with the remaining dough.

# Baklava

The jury is out as to whether this dish originated in Turkey or Greece, but wherever it came from, if you have a sweet tooth, you will love this sweet and syrupy dessert.

**Servings:** 48

**Total Time:** 1hour 15mins

**Ingredients:**

- ½ cup granulated sugar
- 1½ pounds walnuts (finely chopped)
- ⅛ tsp ground cloves
- ½ tsp ground cinnamon
- 1 pound butter (melted, divided)
- 2 (16 ounce) packages frozen phyllo dough (thawed)

**Syrup:**

- 1 cup Greek honey
- 2 cups water
- 2 cups granulated sugar
- 1 tbsp orange peel (grated)

**Directions:**

1. In a small-size bowl, combine the sugar, walnuts, cloves, and cinnamon. Put to one side.
2. Lightly brush a 15x10x1" baking pan with butter.
3. Unroll 1 package of the dough out and cut the stack into 10½ x9" rectangle. Repeat with the remaining dough and discard any scraps.
4. Line the bottom of the prepared baking pan with 2 sheets of phyllo dough (sheets will slightly overlap). Brush lightly with butter. Repeat the layers 14 times, while keeping the dough you aren't using covered with a damp tea towel until you are ready to use. This will prevent it from drying out.
5. Spread 2 cups of the walnut-clove mixture over the dough. Top with 5 layers of dough, brushing with between each dough sheet.
6. Spread with the remaining walnut-clove mixture and top with 1 layer of dough, and brush with butter. Repeat 14 times.
7. Cut into 2½" squares and slice each square diagonally in half. Brush with the remaining butter.
8. Bake in the oven at 350 degrees F until golden, for 40-45 minutes.

9.  For the syrup: In a pan, bring the Greek honey, water, sugar, and orange peel to boil.

10. Turn the heat down and simmer for approximately 10 minutes.

11. Strain the syrup, remove and discard the orange peel and set aside until tepid.

12. Pour the syrup over the baklava and serve.

# Cherry Clafoutis

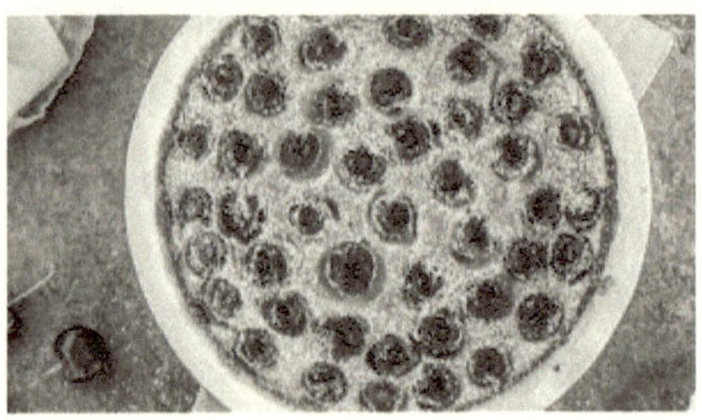

This decadent French dessert is sharp, juicy, and tart. Serve warm with cream for a fantastic finale to a dinner party or special occasion meal.

**Servings:** 4-6

**Total Time:** 1hour 5mins

**Ingredients:**

- 2 ounces plain flour
- ½ tsp baking powder
- 3 large free-range eggs
- 2 ounces sugar
- 1¼ cups milk
- ½ tsp vanilla essence
- ½ tbsp unsalted butter (at room temperature)
- 1 tbsp sugar
- 10½ ounces sour morello cherries (pitted)
- Icing sugar (for dusting)
- Cream (to serve, optional)

**Directions:**

1. Preheat the main oven to 355 degrees F.
2. In a food blender or processor, combine the flour with the baking powder, eggs, sugar, milk, and vanilla essence until entirely smooth. Set aside for 20-30 minutes.
3. In the meantime, grease a round 10" baking pan with softened butter and scatter the sugar over the top.
4. Dot the morello cherries around the base of the dish and transfer to the oven for 5 minutes to allow the fruit to start to soften.
5. Remove the baking dish from the oven.
6. Pour the batter over the top to just cover the cherries. Return the dish to the oven and bake for approximately 30-35 minutes, until golden and puffy.
7. Dust the dessert with icing sugar and ser warm, with cream.

# Chocolate Salami

This rich, chocolatey dessert is popular in both Italy and Portugal. It has taste and texture and is the perfect sweet treat to serve with an afternoon or morning espresso.

**Servings:** 8-10

**Total Time:** 8hours 20mins

**Ingredients:**

- 7 ounces dark chocolate
- 3 ounces unsalted butter (room temperature)
- ⅓ cup sugar
- 2 eggs
- ½ tsp vanilla essence
- 7 ounces Marie tea cookies (any brand, broken up)
- 2 tbsp powdered sugar

**Directions:**

1. Melt together the dark chocolate and butter using a double boiler. Stir until silky.
2. In a second bowl, combine the sugar with the eggs and vanilla.
3. Gradually add the egg mixture to the dark chocolate mixture is entirely smooth. Remove from the heat and fold in the broken-up cookies. Set the mixture aside for approximately 10 minutes. This will help you to form the mixture into shapes later.
4. Cut 2 sheets of parchment paper.
5. Evenly divide the now cooled mixture between the 2 sheets.
6. Tightly roll the mixture into a log shape of approximately 2½" long.
7. Twist the ends of the parchment paper and tie each end with kitchen string. Transfer to the fridge overnight.
8. To Serve: Wrap the chocolate log and scatter the powdered sugar over a clean work surface. Roll the log in the sugar, lightly dusting the outside.
9. Slice, serve, and enjoy.

# Churros with Chocolate Sauce

Crisp and golden, these donut-like Spanish churros rolled in cinnamon sugar and dipped in a creamy dark chocolate sauce are sure to make you a very popular host.

**Servings:** 4

**Total Time:** 20mins

**Ingredients:**

**Coating:**

- ¼ cup caster sugar
- 2 tsp ground cinnamon

**Churros:**

- 1 cup plain white flour
- 1 tsp baking powder
- Pinch of salt
- 1 tbsp olive oil
- 1 cup boiled water
- 2 cups oil (to fry)

**Chocolate Sauce:**

- ½ cup dark chocolate chips
- ½ cup heavy cream

**Directions:**

1. In a bowl, combine the sugar with the cinnamon. Set to one side.
2. In a second bowl, combine the flour with the baking powder and salt.
3. Add the oil and water and mix until just combined to cream a thick batter.
4. Transfer the dough to a piping bag fitted with a star tip ⅓" nozzle. Allow to cool while the oil is heating.
5. Over moderate-high heat, heat the oil in a deep-sided skillet to 340 degrees F,
6. In batches of 3-4, pipe 6" lengths of the dough into the hot oil. Aim to achieve a total yield of 8-10.
7. Fry in the hot oil until golden while occasionally rolling for 2-3 minutes.
8. Transfer the churros onto a kitchen paper towel-lined plate.
9. For the chocolate sauce: Add the dark chocolate chips to the heavy cream in a microwave-safe bowl and, in 30-second increments, melt while stirring between increments until silky smooth.
10. Roll the churros evenly in sugar and serve with the chocolate sauce.

# Cocoa Rose Malabi

This creamy Israeli pudding is sweetened with date honey and delicately flavored and fragranced with rosewater.

**Servings:** 6

**Total Time:** 15mins

**Ingredients:**

- 4 cups almond milk (divided)
- ¼ cup cocoa powder
- ⅓ cup date honey
- ½ cup cornstarch
- 1 tbsp rosewater

**Directions:**

1. In a large-size microwave-safe bowl, whisk 3½ cups with the milk along with the cocoa powder, and honey, and heat on high for 2 minutes.
2. In a small-size bowl, whisk the cornstarch with the remaining almond milk.
3. Whisk the cornstarch mixture into the warmed milk-cocoa powder mixture.
4. Return to the microwave for an additional 4-6 minutes, whisking every couple of minutes until the mixture reaches a pudding-like consistency.
5. Remove from the microwave and whisk in the rosewater.
6. Pour the dessert into decorative dessert cups and place them in the fridge to cool.
7. Enjoy.

# Croatian Plum Dumplings

These fruity little dumplings, or 'Knedle sa Sljivama,' are soft and delicious, the perfect wintertime comfort food.

**Servings:** 16

**Total Time:** 50mins

**Ingredients:**

- 2 eggs (beaten)
- 3 potatoes (peeled, boiled, mashed, cooled)
- ½ tsp salt
- 1½ cups all-purpose flour
- 16 white sugar cubes
- 16 damson plums (pitted)
- ¼ cup butter

- ¼ cup breadcrumbs
- Powdered sugar (for serving)

**Directions:**

1. Combine the beaten egg, mashed potato, and salt in a bowl. Add the flour and mix until incorporated.
2. Insert a sugar cube into the center of each pitted plum.
3. Bring a deep pot of salty water to a boil.
4. Flour your clean hands, and take 1/16th of the dough, flatten it in the palm of your hand. Place a stuffed plum in the center and form the sides of the dough up around the plum to cover. Drop the dumpling into the boiling water. Repeat with the remaining dough and plums.
5. Boil the dumplings for 20 minutes.
6. In the meantime, melt the butter in a skillet over moderate heat. Add the breadcrumbs and sauté until browned.
7. Remove the dumplings from the boiling water and transfer to a serving plate. Spoon over the sautéed breadcrumbs and butter. Dust with powdered sugar and serve.

# Egyptian Sweet Pastry Dessert

Umm Ali is a traditional pastry dessert and is very similar to bread pudding. It features puff pastry with almonds, raisins, and coconut.

**Servings:** 6

**Total Time:** 25mins

**Ingredients:**

- 1 sheet puff pastry
- ¼ cup sliced almonds
- ¼ cup coconut chips
- ¼ cup raisins
- ⅛ cup granulated sugar
- 1 cup whole milk
- 1 cup half-and-half

**Directions:**

1. Bake the puff pastry according to the package instructions and cool to room temperature before tearing into bite-size pieces and arranging in a 9" square casserole dish.
2. Preheat the main oven to 425 degrees F.
3. Scatter the almonds along with the coconut chips, raisins, and sugar evenly over the torn pastry.
4. Pour in the milk and half and half, making sure it evenly and entirely coats the pastry.
5. Bake in the preheated oven until bubbling and toasted.
6. Serve and enjoy.

# Greek Christmas Cookies

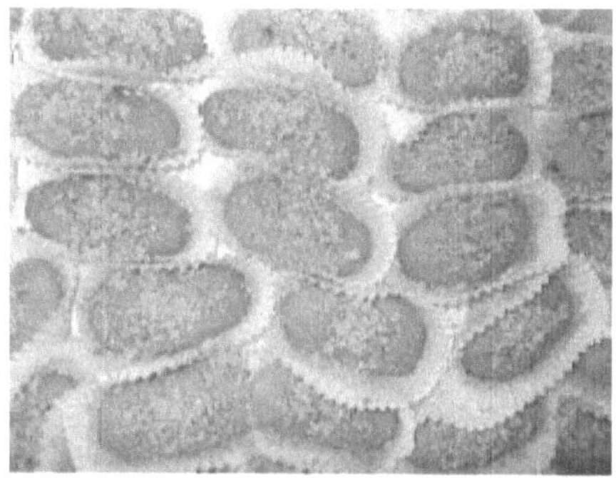

Kourabiedes are melt-in-the-mouth cookies that are enjoyed all over Greece during the holidays.

**Servings:** 40

**Total Time:** 1hour 10mins

**Ingredients:**

- 1 pound butter (room temperature)
- ½ cup powdered sugar
- 1 egg yolk
- 1 tbsp brandy
- 1 tsp vanilla essence
- 5 cups flour
- 1 tsp baking powder
- 1 cup slivered almonds (lightly roasted)
- 6-7 cups powdered sugar

**Directions:**

1. Preheat the main oven to 350 degrees F. Using parchment paper line baking sheets.
2. Add the butter along with the powdered sugar to the bowl of a stand mixer and on medium speed beat for 10-15 minutes, until light and fluffy.
3. Add the egg yolk, brandy, and vanilla essence. Beat until entirely combined.
4. Sift the flour and baking powder into a mixing bowl. A little at a time, add the flour mixture to the butter mixture. Next, add the almonds and beat until incorporated.
5. Roll the dough out into 1 tablespoonful-size balls.
6. Arrange the balls on the baking sheet and bake in the oven for 10 minutes. Rotate the baking sheets and continue baking for 10 minutes.
7. Evenly spread approximately half of the remaining powdered sugar in a deep baking pan.
8. Remove the cookies from the oven and gently place each one in the powdered sugar.
9. Cover the cookies with the remaining sugar and allow to completely cool before serving.

# Greek Fried Doughnuts

These little golden doughnuts are known in Greece as loukoumades. They are served dripping in cinnamon, honey, and sesame seeds.

**Servings:** 6-8

**Total Time:** 4hours 30mins

**Ingredients:**

- 1 sachet dry yeast
- 2 cups warm water
- 1 tsp granulated sugar
- 4 cups flour
- 1 tsp salt
- Olive oil
- Honey, cinnamon, and sesame seeds (for serving)

**Directions:**

1. Dissolve the yeast in half of the warm water. Add the sugar and 1½ cups of the flour to the mixture. Beat until smooth. Cover with a dishcloth and set aside in a warm place until it is double its original size.
2. To the mixture, add the remaining 1 cup of warm water, salt, and remaining flour. Cover again and set aside to rise for 1½ hours.
3. Heat 3" of olive oil in a deep pan over moderately low heat until it is hot but not smoking. Drop 10 small spoonfuls of dough into the oil at a time. Fry until the dough is golden brown and puffed.
4. Transfer the cooked loukoumades to a plate covered with kitchen paper.
5. Serve the cooked doughnuts drizzled with a generous amount of honey and a sprinkling of cinnamon and sesame seeds.

# Halva

Semolina-based Greek halva is a traditional dessert that is also popular in South Asia and the Middle East.

**Servings:** 20

**Total Time:** 20mins

**Ingredients:**

- 4 cups water
- 8 cups sugar
- 8 sticks of cinnamon
- 8 cloves
- 1 cup of Greek honey
- 1 cup Greek extra-virgin olive oil
- 1 tbsp ground cinnamon
- 2 cups semolina
- 1 cup walnuts

**Directions:**

1.  In a pan, add 4 cups of water along with the sugar, cinnamon sticks, cloves, and bring to boil for 5 minutes. Turn the heat off and add the Greek honey.

2.  In a deep-sided pot, on moderate-high heat, add the olive oil along with the semolina. Continually stir with a wooden spoon until the color changes from golden blond to golden brown.

3.  As soon as the color changes, add 1 tablespoon of ground cinnamon, and stir well.

4.  Gradually and slowly add a small amount of the syrup to the semolina.

5.  On moderate-low heat, continuously stir until the mixture begins to thicken. Add the walnuts and stir.

6.  Transfer the mixture to a cake pan and allow to cool.

7.  Turn the halva onto a cake platter and sprinkle with cinnamon.

# Italian Cake

The addition of buttermilk makes this sponge super moist and fluffy. This cake is ideal for any celebration or large get-together.

**Servings:** 12

**Total Time:** 1hours 30mins

**Ingredients:**

- Butter and flour (for cake tins)

**Cake:**

- ½ cup shortening
- ½ cup butter (at room temperature)
- 2 cups granulated sugar
- 5 eggs
- 1 tsp vanilla essence
- ¼ tsp salt
- 2 cups all-purpose flour
- 1 tsp bicarbonate of soda
- 1 cup buttermilk
- ½ cup shredded, sweetened coconut
- 1 cup pecans (chopped)

**Frosting:**

- ¾ cups butter (at room temperature)
- 11 ounces cream cheese (at room temperature)
- 3¾ cups powdered sugar
- 1 tsp vanilla essence
- 1 cup pecans (roughly chopped)

**Directions:**

1. Preheat the main oven to 350 degrees F. Grease and flour three 9" cake tins.
2. Beat together the shortening, butter, and sugar until fluffy. Mix in the eggs one at a time. Finally, mix in the vanilla essence.
3. In a second bowl, sift together the salt, flour, and bicarb of soda. Fold the dry ingredients into the wet in batches, alternating with splashes of buttermilk. When the batter is combined, fold in the coconut and pecans.
4. Pour the batter equally into the 3 cake tins. Place in the oven and bake for just over 20 minutes. Allow to cool before removing the cakes from the tins.
5. In the meantime, prepare the frosting. Beat together the butter and cream cheese until fluffy. Beat in the powdered sugar and vanilla essence.
6. Spread the frosting between the cake layers before stacking and cover the outside. Press the chopped pecans onto the sides of the cake.
7. Chill until ready to serve.

# Karyoka

These Turkish chocolate-covered chestnuts are a pop-in-the-mouth luxury confection to serve with after-dinner coffee or liqueurs.

**Servings:** 16

**Total Time:** 1hour

**Ingredients:**

- 1 pound chestnuts
- ½ cup confectioner's sugar
- 2-4 tbsp heavy cream
- 1 pound 14 ounces bitter, dark chocolate
- 2 tbsp pistachios (ground)

**Directions:**

1. First, prepare the chestnuts. Use a sharp knife and slice each nut crosswise into the outer hull and also penetrate the inner hull.

2. Add the nuts to a large pan and pour in sufficient water to thoroughly cover the chestnuts. Bring to boil and allow the nuts to boil with a partially covered lid for approximately 20 minutes, until very tender.

3. Once the nuts are tender, drain and rinse under cold running water.

4. Use the sharp paring knife to remove the nut's outer shell along with the inner brown membrane. Take care to remove all the membranes and avoid leaving any of the small pieces.

5. First, put 2 cups of the boiled and peeled nuts, confectioner's sugar, and 2 tablespoons of heavy cream in a processor and on high, pulse until combined.

6. Little by little, continue to add the cream processing until you have a dough-like puree that isn't sticky. Remove the puree from the processor and form it into a ball-shape and transfer it to the fridge to rest for half an hour.

7.  Melt together the bitter chocolate and 1 tbsp heavy cream using a microwave, stir until silky.

8.  Cover a baking sheet with wax paper.

9.  Break off chestnut-size pieces of the chilled dough and roll into balls.

10. Dip each ball into the melted chocolate to evenly coat. Continue until all of the dough is used.

11. Arrange the balls on the prepared baking sheet. Scatter over the pistachios while the chocolate is still wet.

12. Chill for 20 minutes until set before serving.

# King Cake

The original recipe for King Cake hails from Southern France and is centuries old. The cake was traditionally served on January 6th. An item (or fever) was hidden and baked in the cake. These were originally broad beans, but as time went on, they were replaced by porcelain figures or even cartoon characters. This recipe is a modern take on a traditional King Cake.

**Servings:** 10-12

**Total Time:** 3hours

**Ingredients:**

- 17 ounces flour (sieved)
- 3½ ounces sugar
- 1 tsp salt
- 3¼ tsp bread yeast
- ½ cup milk
- 2 tbsp orange blossom water
- 3 whole eggs
- 3½ ounces red candied fruits
- 1 egg yolk
- Powdered sugar (to garnish)
- Red candied fruits (to garnish)
- 5¼ ounces butter (softened)

**Directions:**

1. In a bowl, combine the flour with sugar and the salt.

2. Create a hole in the middle of the mixture, and a little at a time add the yeast, the milk, the orange blossom water, and the eggs, mixing thoroughly.

3. Knead the butter into the mixture for 5-10 minutes, until you create a smooth paste that doesn't stick to the hands.

4. Form the mixture into a dough and allow to rest for 15 minutes. Cover with a clean, tea towel and allow it to rise to three times its original volume.

5. Add the diced candied fruits and form the mixture into a circle. Join the 2 ends to create a round crown shape. Here, a figurine would typically be hidden, but you can skip this stage.

6. Cover with a clean tea towel and allow to rise for 75 minutes in a warm environment (a switched off, warm oven is ideal).

7. Approximately 15 minutes before the end of the rising period, preheat the main oven to 355 degrees F.

8. Glaze the surface with an egg yolk and lightly dust with icing sugar.

9. Place on a parchment-lined baking tray and bake in the oven for 30-35 minutes.

10. Remove from the oven and decorate with red candied fruits.

# Libyan Semolina and Date Cake with Syrup

This traditional cake from Libya flavored with aromatic and warm spices and drenched in sweet honey, and lemon syrup will have everyone coming back for more.

**Servings:** 8-10

**Total Time:** 7hours 30mins

**Ingredients:**

**Date Filling:**

- 3 tbsp sunflower oil
- 1½ pounds dates (pitted, chopped)
- ⅛ tsp ground cloves
- 1 tsp ground cinnamon

**Cake:**

- 2 pound fine or medium semolina
- 1 pound granulated sugar
- 2 tsp baking powder
- 1 cup sunflower oil
- ¼ cup water
- Blanched almonds (to garnish)

**Syrup:**

- 1 cup sugar
- ½ cup water
- 1 cup honey
- 2-3 tbsp freshly squeezed lemon juice

**Directions:**

1. Over low heat, combine the oil and dates in a frying pan or skillet and while continuously stirring cook for approximately 20 minutes, or until a thick paste-like consistency.
2. Take the pan off the heat and stir in the cloves, followed by the cinnamon. Set aside to cool.
3. In a bowl, mix the semolina, sugar, baking powder, sunflower oil, and water into a thick batter.
4. Transfer half of the batter into a 12" square cake tin.
5. Add the date filling to the pan, gently pressing it into the corners of the cake tin to cover the batter.
6. Pour in the remaining batter and evenly smooth out the surface.
7. Lightly score the surface of the cake in 2" diamond shapes.
8. Place 1 blanched almond in the middle of each diamond shape.
9. Put the cake on the middle shelf of the oven and bake at 350 degrees F for 45 minutes.
10. Next, prepare the syrup. Add the sugar, water, honey, and lemon juice to a pan and over low heat, simmer for 10 minutes, while frequently stirring.
11. Remove the cake from the oven.

12. Pour the hot syrup over the cake and allow it to soak
    in.

13. Stand for 6 hours before serving.

# Madeleines

These mouth-watering French fancies are small shell-shaped cakes. Be warned, though; you won't be able to stop at just one!

**Servings:** 6

**Total Time:** 25mins

**Ingredients:**

- ¼ tsp baking powder
- 5 ounces all-purpose flour (sieved)
- 3 eggs
- 1 egg yolk
- 5 ounces sugar
- ½ tsp freshly squeezed lemon juice
- Lemon zest from ½ lemon
- 5 ounces unsalted butter, melted

**Directions:**

1. In a bowl, combine the baking powder with the sieved flour.
2. Preheat the main oven to 400 degrees F. Lightly grease a Madeleine baking pan with butter.
3. Using an electric hand beater, beat the eggs, yolk, and sugar until foamy and thickened.
4. Add the lemon juice followed by the lemon zest and blend to combine.
5. Fold in flour and with a spatula mix thoroughly.
6. Next, fold in the melted butter, stirring until entirely incorporated.

# Maltese Ice Cream

Now you, too, can enjoy this traditional Maltese ice cream. It is often served on the beautiful island of Malta as a sweet dessert for special occasions and celebrations.

**Servings:** 2-4

**Total Time:** 1hour 30mins

**Ingredients:**

- 2 (12 ounce) can evaporated milk (divided)
- ½ cup sugar
- 1 stick of cinnamon
- Grated rind of 1 lemon
- ¼ heavy cream
- ½ tsp vanilla extract
- ½ cup of nuts (crushed, of choice)

**Directions:**

1. Add 1 can of the evaporated milk along with the sugar, cinnamon stick and grated lemon rind to a pan and bring to boil. Turn the heat down to a simmer for approximately 10 minutes.
2. Pour the mixture through a fine-mesh sieve into a stainless steel bowl. Remove and discard the lemon rind and stick of cinnamon.
3. Stir in the remaining can of evaporated milk along with the heavy cream and vanilla.
4. Transfer to the freezer for half an hour.
5. Pour the mixture into your ice cream maker and churn according to manufacturer instructions and to your preferred consistency.
6. Serve the ice cream with the crushed nuts.

# Moroccan Fruitcake

Ras el Hanout is a Moroccan seasoning, and in this recipe, it transforms a family fruitcake into a baking triumph. Serve toasted and buttered.

**Servings:** 6-8

**Total Time:** 9hours 30mins

**Ingredients:**

- ½ cup dried currants
- ½ cup raisins
- ½ dried figs (cut into ½" dice)
- ½ cup dried apricots (cut into ½" dice)
- ½ cup prunes (cut into ½" dice)
- 1 cup Assam tea (brewed, hot)
- 1½ cups self-rising flour
- 2 tsp Ras el Hanout
- ¼ tsp Kosher salt
- ¾ cup packed light brown sugar
- 1 large-size egg (lightly beaten)
- Whole milk
- Salted butter (room temperature, to serve)

**Directions:**

1. In a bowl, combine the currants with the raisins, dried figs, dried apricots, and prunes.
2. Pour the tea over the dried fruits and cover. Allow to stand in a cool environment overnight; this will help the fruit to plump up and absorb the flavor of the tea.
3. Preheat the main oven to 375 degrees F. Using parchment paper line an 8½x4½" loaf pan, allowing an overhang of 1½" on the longest sides.
4. Into a bowl, sift the flour along with the Ras el Hanout and salt into a mixing bowl. Add the brown sugar and stir in the dried fruit mixture along with any liquids along with the egg, mixing until combined. The batter should be dropping consistency, as in it should easily drop off a spoon. If too thick, you may add a drop of milk.
5. Transfer the batter to the prepared loaf pan and bake for 50-55 minutes, until springy to the touch.
6. Allow the cake to cool while in the pan for 10 minutes before inverting onto a wire baking rack to completely cool before slicing and serving.
7. Alternatively, toast and spread with butter.
8. This cake can be well wrapped in kitchen wrap and stored at room temperature for up to 72 days.

# Moroccan Spiced Fruit Salad

Fresh fruit and nuts sweetened with honey and served with warm cinnamon are proof positive that there is a lot more to Moroccan cuisine than tagines and couscous.

**Servings:** 4

**Total Time:** 4mins

**Ingredients:**

- 4 sweet, ripe oranges (peeled, seeded, cut into bite-sized pieces)
- ½ cup pomegranate arils
- 1 tbsp orange zest
- ½ cup almonds (chopped)
- ¼ cup pistachios (chopped)
- 3 tbsp runny honey
- 1 tbsp water
- Cinnamon (serve)
- Orange zest (grated, to serve)

**Directions:**

1. In a large mixing bowl, combine the pieces of orange with the pomegranate arils, orange zest, almonds, and pistachios. Stir to incorporate entirely.
2. In a small-size microwave-safe bowl, in the microwave, warm the honey along with the water for 30 seconds. Stir to combine.
3. Pour the warm honey over the fruit and nut mixture and toss until evenly and well coated.
4. Garnish with ground cinnamon and grated orange zest.

# North African Orange Dessert

Exotic, easy, and refreshing; this sweet North African dessert is an ideal after-dinner dessert to enjoy mid-week. What's more, it makes a great breakfast dish, too.

**Servings:** 2

**Total Time:** 10mins

**Ingredients:**

- ¼ cup orange juice (freshly pressed)
- 1½ orange blossom water
- 1 tbsp runny honey
- 3 medium-sized oranges (carefully peeled, seeded, and cut into round slices)
- 1 tsp cinnamon
- 7 mint leaves (to garnish)

**Directions:**

1. In a small-size bowl, combine the orange juice with the orange blossom water and honey. Set aside in a cool environment.
2. Arrange the slices of orange in a serving dish.
3. Sprinkle the juice-water evenly over the top.
4. Sprinkle with cinnamon and decorate with mint.
5. Serve at once.

# Panna Cotta with Fresh Berries

Italia berry panna cotta has a velvet-smooth texture and is topped with a chilled berry sauce for a creamy and decadent dinner-party treat.

**Servings:** 6

**Total Time:** 3hours 30mins

**Ingredients:**

**Panna Cotta:**

- 3 cups whole milk
- 1 (¼ ounce) envelope unflavored, powdered gelatin
- ⅓ cup granulated sugar
- ½ tsp almond essence
- Nonstick cooking spray

**Berry Sauce:**

- ½ cup granulated sugar
- 1 cup water
- 2 cups unsweetened, frozen mixed berries
- ½ cup port wine
- ½ cup fresh blueberries
- ½ cup fresh raspberries

**Directions:**

1. First, prepare the panna cotta. Add the milk to a small saucepan and sprinkle over the gelatin. Set aside to stand for 60 seconds. Place the pan over low heat, warm the mixture while stirring until the gelatin has dissolved.

2. Add the granulated sugar, when it has dissolved, stir in the almond essence.

3. Pour the mixture equally into 6 small ramekins spritzed with nonstick spray. Chill until set.

4. In the meantime, prepare the berry sauce. Add the sugar and water to a small saucepan, place over moderate heat and bring the mixture to a boil.

5. Add the frozen berries to the pan along with the port. Return the mixture to the boil before reducing the heat to a simmer.

6. Continue cooking for 5 minutes without a lid. Mash then strain the berries, discard all seeds, and reserve all juice.

7. Return the seedless berry juice to the saucepan and bring to a boil. Turn the heat down to a simmer. Cook for several minutes until the liquid is reduced to around ¾ of a cup. Pour the mixture into a bowl, cover with plastic wrap, and chill until cool.

8. Turn the panna cottas out onto individual serving plates and spoon over an equal amount of the chilled berry sauce and berries.

# Pears in Red Wine

These boozy pears cooked in red wine, sweetened with brown sugar and flavored with warm cinnamon, make the best-ever dessert.

**Servings:** 4

**Total Time:** 1hour 10mins

**Ingredients:**

- ½ fresh lemon
- 4 medium, stalk-on, ripe pears (peeled)
- 2 sticks of cinnamon
- 4½ ounces brown sugar
- ¼ cup port
- 1¾ cups red wine

**Directions:**

1. Zest and juice ½ a lemon.

2. Sprinkle the lemon juice over the pears; this will prevent them from browning.

3. Add the cinnamon, lemon zest, sugar, port, and red wine in a large pan and simmer on moderate-low heat until the sugar melts.

4. Next, place the pears in the pan and cover, boil for an additional 15 minutes or until fork-tender, and not mushy.

5. Remove the pears from the pan and arrange on a serving plate.

6. Pour the wine into the liquid, and uncovered over moderate-low heat, boil for 40 minutes, until a thickened syrup-like consistency.

7. Pour the syrup over the pears, allow the syrup to slightly cool and serve.

# Pumpkin Dreams

Portuguese fried pumpkin cakes or Sonhos de Abóbora consist of crunchy fried dough with a creamy sweet pumpkin filling, coated in cinnamon and sugar.

**Servings:** 4

**Total Time:** 25mins

**Ingredients:**

- 1 cup milk
- 1 cup water
- 8 tbsp vegetable oil
- Pinch of salt
- Zest of 1 orange
- 10½ ounces flour
- 8¾ ounces pumpkin puree
- 4 medium-size eggs
- Cinnamon (to roll)
- Sugar (to roll)

**Directions:**

1. In a pan, bring the milk, water, oil, salt, and orange zest to boil. Add the flour and mix thoroughly until the mixture pulls away from the sides.
2. Remove the pan from the heat, and transfer to a bowl and allow the mixture to cool to room temperature.
3. Gradually add the pumpkin puree mixing thoroughly between additions.
4. One at a time, add the eggs and beat well.
5. Using 2 spoons, make large oval-shape pieces of dough and deep fry in hot oil until the dough is golden brown.
6. Remove from the pan and place on kitchen paper towels.
7. Roll at once in cinnamon and sugar to evenly coat.

# Revani

Revani, a cake from Albania, is made using cornmeal and is drenched with a sugar topping. Its texture is quite like a regular sponge cake but denser, thanks to the plain yogurt.

**Servings:** 8

**Total Time:** 45mis

**Ingredients**

**Syrup:**

- 2 cups sugar
- 1¾ cups water
- 1 tbsp freshly squeezed lemon juice

**Cake:**

- 4 eggs
- ¾ cup plain yogurt
- ¾ cup olive oil
- ¾ cup sugar
- 2¾ cups all-purpose flour
- 1¾ cups cornmeal
- 3 tbsp baking powder
- ½ cup pistachios (crushed, to garnish)
- ¼ cup confectioner's sugar (to garnish)
- Fresh mint leaves (to garnish)
- 1 lemon (sliced, to garnish)

**Directions:**

1. To prepare the syrup: In a pan, bring the sugar and water to boil while frequently stirring. Boil for 10-15 minutes, removing from the heat as soon as it starts to thicken. Add the lemon juice and allow it to cool.
2. Preheat the main oven to 350 degrees F.
3. In a mixing bowl, combine the eggs with the yogurt, olive oil, and sugar and mix.
4. Add the flour, cornmeal, and baking powder until thoroughly blended.
5. Pour into a 9x12" greased pan.
6. Bake in the oven for half an hour, until golden.
7. Slice into squares.
8. Pour the syrup over the squares and allow to soak into the cake.
9. Garnish with crushed pistachios, confectioner's sugar, fresh mint leaves and a slice of lemon.

# Rosewater and Pistachio Ice Cream

This delicate dessert combines the classic Turkish flavors of fragrant rosewater and delicate pistachios.

**Servings:** 6

**Total Time:** 3hours 30mins

**Ingredients:**

- 1 cup heavy cream
- 1½ cups whole milk
- ¾ cup granulated sugar
- 1 tbsp cornflour
- 1 tbsp rosewater
- ½ cup Greek yogurt
- 5¼ toasted pistachios (chopped)

**Directions:**

1. Combine the heavy cream, whole milk, and granulated sugar in a saucepan and place over moderate heat and bring to a simmer while stirring.
2. In a small bowl, stir together the cornflour and rosewater. Fold this mixture into the cream/milk.
3. Take the pan off the heat and allow the mixture to cool. Fold in the yogurt.
4. Transfer the mixture along with the pistachios to an ice-cream churner and process using manufacturer instructions.
5. Freeze until firm enough to scoop.

# Semolina Cake with Syrup

Like the majority of Cypriot or Greek desserts, this semolina cake is very sweet. A little goes a long way, so slice into small-size squares.

**Servings:** 12

**Total Time:** 3hours 10mins

**Ingredients:**

**Cake Mixture:**

- 4 eggs
- ¾ cup sugar
- 1 cup milk
- 1 cup vegetable oil
- 1 tsp baking powder
- 2-3 drops rosewater
- 17 ounces semolina
- A handful of almonds (halved)

**Sugar Syrup:**

- 3 cups caster sugar
- 2 cups boiling water
- 1 tsp freshly squeezed lemon juice
- ½ tsp rosewater
- 3 sticks of cinnamon

**Directions:**

1. For the cake mixture: Crack the eggs into a large-size mixing bowl, and whisk.
2. Add the sugar along with the milk, vegetable oil, baking powder, and rosewater and whisk.
3. Next, add the semolina and mix thoroughly.
4. Transfer the mixture to a deep baking tray. Ideally, the mixture should be 3" deep.
5. Arrange the halves of almonds in attractive rows across the surface of the mixture.
6. Place in the oven at 340 degrees F for 30-40 minutes, until golden or springy to the touch. Allow to slightly cool.
7. In the meantime, make the syrup.
8. In a pan, combine the sugar with the boiling water, fresh lemon juice, rosewater, and sticks of cinnamon.
9. Bring to boil before simmering for approximately 10 minutes. The syrup should not be very thick.
10. When the cake is just warm, cut into 2" squares.
11. Pour the sugar over the squares and allow to soak for 2 hours.
12. Serve at room temperature.

# Sicilian Lemon Tart

This Sicilian tart uses three varieties of lemon; curd, limoncello liqueur, and zest for a big, bold flavor.

**Servings:** 8

**Total Time:** 2hours 50mins

**Ingredients:**

- 8 ounces mascarpone cheese
- 2½ tbsp limoncello
- Zest of 1 lemon
- 2 tsp vanilla essence
- 1 cup lemon curd
- 1 (9") ready-made sweet tart crust
- ½ pint heavy cream

- 1 tbsp powdered sugar

**Directions:**

1. Preheat the main oven to 300 degrees F.
2. Using an electric whisk, beat the mascarpone cheese with the limoncello, lemon zest, and 1 tsp of vanilla essence. Add the lemon curd and continue to mix until incorporated.
3. Pour the mixture into the tart crust. Place in the oven and bake for 15 minutes, turn the pie 180 degrees, and bake for another 10-15 minutes until the tart is just puffy with a slightly jiggly center.
4. Allow the tart to cool completely before transferring to the refrigerator for a couple of hours.
5. Just before you are ready to serve, prepare the whipped cream.
6. Using an electric whisk, whip the cream with the powdered sugar until it can hold firm peaks. Dollop the cream on top of the pie, slice, and serve.

# Slovenian Apple Pie

Rich, buttery pastry encases caramelized cinnamon apples. Slovenian apple pie differs from the classic British variety, in that the apples are grated and combined with breadcrumbs, rather than left whole.

**Servings:** 8

**Total Time:** 1hour

**Ingredients:**

**Crust:**

- 2 tsp baking powder
- 2½ cups all-purpose flour
- ¾ cup confectioner's sugar
- ¼ tsp sea salt
- Yolks of 2 medium eggs
- ⅔ cup unsalted butter (at room temperature)
- 6 tbsp sour cream
- ½ tsp vanilla bean paste

**Filling:**

- 3-4 large apples (peeled, cored, grated)
- ¼ cup granulated sugar
- 2 tbsp brown sugar
- 1 tbsp fresh lemon juice
- 1 tsp cinnamon
- 2 tbsp breadcrumbs

**Directions:**

1. Sift the baking powder, all-purpose flour, confectioner's sugar, and sea salt together into a bowl.

2. In a second bowl, beat together the egg yolks and butter until creamy. Next, beat in the sour cream and vanilla bean paste. Add the flour to the mixture in three batches, beating well between each addition until the mixture comes together in a soft dough. Flatten then cover the dough with plastic wrap and chill until ready to use later.

3. Prepare the apple mixture. Add the grated apple, granulated sugar, brown sugar, lemon juice, cinnamon, and breadcrumbs. Toss the mixture until combined. Set to one side.

4. Preheat the main oven to 355 degrees F. Line a 9" springform tin with parchment.

5. Divide the dough into two portions, one a little larger than the other.

6. On a floured worktop, roll out the larger piece of dough, then arrange it in the pie tin, pat it 2cm up the sides of the tin.

7. Take the apple mixture out of the refrigerator; drain away any water from the bowl. Spoon the apple mixture evenly over the pie crust.

8. Roll out the remaining piece of dough and arrange it over the filling — Tuck in at the edges and make a few small slices on the top.

9. Place the pie in the oven and bake for just over 40 minutes until golden.

10. Allow to cool before removing from the pie tin.

# Spanish Cheesecake

Quesada Pasiega is a dessert typical of Cantabria in Spain. It has a dense pudding-like consistency, and you can serve it either hot or cold. Although not at all like a regular cheesecake, it is delicious and moreish.

**Servings:** 8

**Total Time:** 55mins

**Ingredients:**

- 5 tbsp unsalted butter (room temperature)
- 1 cup sugar
- 2 eggs
- 1 tsp vanilla essence
- 7 ounces ricotta cheese
- Small pinch of salt
- 2 cups whole milk
- 1 cup flour
- 2 tsp lemon zest

**Directions:**

1. Preheat the main oven to 350 degrees F.
2. In a bowl, cream the butter with the sugar and whisk in the eggs and vanilla essence.
3. Beat well and add the ricotta cheese along with a pinch of salt.
4. Beat in the milk, and gradually add the flour.
5. Add the lemon zest and stir to combine.
6. Transfer the mixture into a 9x13" baking dish and bake in the oven for 35-45 minutes or until gently browned and springy to the touch.
7. Allow the cheesecake to cool for a minimum of 15 minutes, until set.

# Spanish Rice Pudding

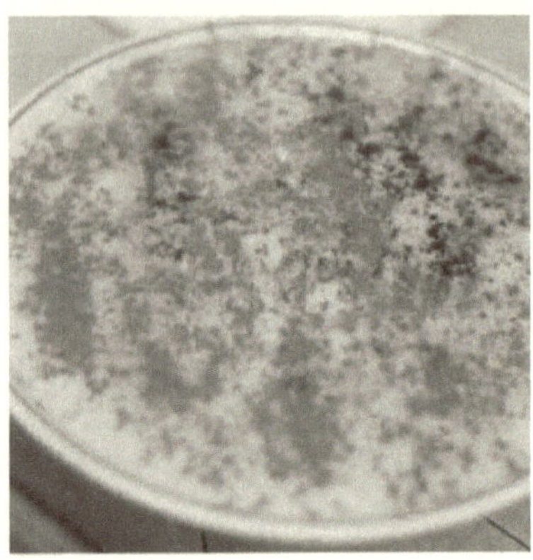

Arroz con Leche is not exclusive to Spain. You can find it not only in Europe but also in Asia and Latin American, but none is more delicious than this recipe.

**Servings:** 4

**Total Time:** 35mins

**Ingredients:**

- 1 cup short-grain rice (rinsed under cold water)
- 1 cinnamon stick
- 1-2 thick slices lemon rind
- 1-quart whole milk
- Pinch of salt
- 1 tsp ground cinnamon
- Sugar (to taste)

**Directions:**

1. Add the rinsed rice to a pan. Pour in sufficient water to just barely cover the rice and set over moderate heat.
2. Add the cinnamon stick along with the lemon rind and continually stir until all of the water is absorbed.
3. Approximately ½ cup at a time pour in the milk, stirring between additions until it absorbs. Continue until you have added all of the milk and continually stir.
4. When the rice is creamy, taste to test the texture is to your preferred level of doneness.
5. Turn the heat off and add a pinch of salt and a pinch of cinnamon.
6. Taste and add sugar to sweeten as needed.
7. Enjoy the rice pudding warm or allow to cool.
8. Garnish with cinnamon and enjoy.

# Stuffed Turkish Apricots

This iconic Turkish dessert is fresh and light, ideal for serving after a rich meat course.

**Servings:** 12

**Total Time:** 45mins

**Ingredients:**

- ½ cup Greek yogurt
- ¼ cup granulated sugar
- ½ tsp rosewater
- ½ tsp lemon zest
- Pinch salt
- 2 cups water
- 2 bay leaves
- 4 green cardamom pods (cracked)
- 1 tbsp fresh lemon juice
- 24 whole-dried apricots
- ¼ cup toasted pistachios (finely chopped)

**Directions:**

1.  In a bowl, stir together the Greek yogurt, 1 teaspoon of the sugar, rosewater, lemon zest, and salt. Chill until ready to use.

2.  Add the water, bay leaves, cardamom pods, lemon juice, and remaining granulated sugar to a small saucepan over moderately low heat and cook while stirring for 2 minutes until the sugar dissolves.

3.  Add the apricots to the pan and bring to a simmer, cook for half an hour, stirring occasionally. The apricots should be tender and plump. Transfer the cooked apricots to a plate and allow it to cool.

4.  Take the bay leaves and cardamom pods out of the pan and return the syrup to the heat. Bring to a boil and cook for 5 minutes until it becomes thick. You should have around 3 tbsp of syrup. Take the syrup off the heat and allow to cool.

5.  Scatter the chopped pistachios onto a plate.

6.  Transfer the chilled Greek yogurt mixture to a piping bag and full each apricot evenly with the mixture. Roll each apricot in the chopped pistachios, transfer to a serving plate. Drizzle the syrup over the apricots before serving.

# Tartufo

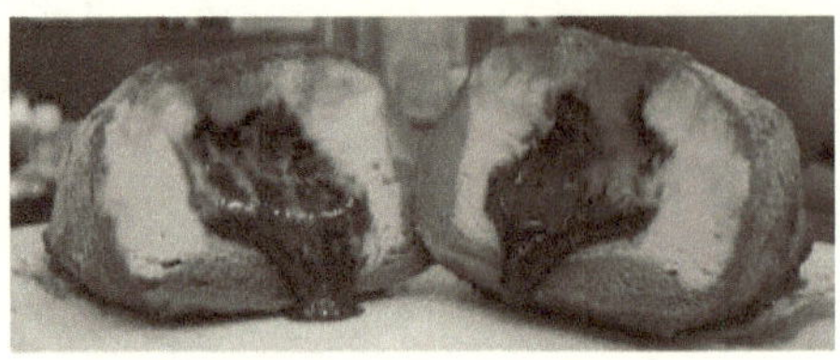

Tartufo is an Italian frozen dessert that originates from Calabria. It tastes as good as it looks and is a lot easier to make than you may think.

**Servings:** 6

**Total Time:** 9hours

**Ingredients:**

- 2 cups chocolate ice cream (softened)
- 1 cup vanilla ice cream (softened)
- 1 cup raspberry or cherry sorbet (softened)
- 10½ ounces dark chocolate (melted)

**Directions:**

1. Fill a 6-cup silicon dome-shape mold full with the chocolate ice cream and transfer to the freezer for 20 minutes, until semi-firm.
2. Scoop some of the ice cream out of the middle of each cup and fill with softened vanilla ice cream. Return to the freezer for approximately 20 minutes until semi-firm.
3. Scoop a small amount of the vanilla ice cream out of the middle of each cup and fill with raspberry sorbet.
4. Transfer the molds to the freezer overnight.
5. Unmold the desserts onto a wire baking rack.
6. Melt the chocolate.
7. Pour the melted chocolate over the top of each dessert and transfer to a plate.
8. Immediately return the Tartufo to the freezer until needed.

# Tunisian Almond Balls

These Almond Balls or Kaber el Louz as they are called in Tunisia, are served for special occasions. Place each ball in a petite four case for the wow factor.

**Servings:** 12

**Total Time:** 35mins

**Ingredients:**

- ¾ cup caster sugar
- 2 tsp vanilla sugar
- 7 tbsp water
- 4 tsp rosewater
- 2½ cups almond meal
- ½ tsp red food coloring
- ½ tsp green food coloring
- Superfine sugar (to garnish)
- Pine nuts (to garnish)

**Directions:**

1. In a small-size pan, combine the sugar with the vanilla sugar.
2. Stir in the water and over moderate heat, cook while occasionally whisking for 10 minutes, or until the sugar is entirely dissolved. Next, whisk in the rosewater.
3. Add the almond meal to a mixing bowl.
4. Using a wooden spoon stir in the syrup.
5. As soon as the dough comes together, on a clean work surface lightly dusted with almond meal, knead until smooth.
6. Divide the dough into 3 even-sized portions. Take the first pieces and knead in the red food coloring, knead green coloring into the second, and leave the third, plain.
7. Roll each portion of dough into a ¾" wide rope.
8. Arrange the ropes side by side and braid together.
9. Push the braids together to seal before cutting into 1" long pieces.
10. Roll each one into a ball.
11. Sprinkle some superfine sugar onto a shallow dish.
12. Roll each dough ball in the sugar to evenly coat.
13. Garnish with pine nuts and serve.

# Turkish Carrot Delight

Cezerye is a sweet confectionery made up of carrots, nuts, and sugar flavored with cinnamon. In Turkey, many believe it to be an aphrodisiac.

**Servings:** 12-15

**Time:** 1hour

**Ingredients:**

- 2 pounds 2 ounces carrots (peeled)
- 2 cups granulated sugar
- 1 cup hazelnuts (crumbled)
- ½ tsp cinnamon
- Desiccated coconut flakes

**Directions:**

1.  Cut each carrot into 4 evenly sized pieces. Add the carrots to a pan and cover with water until they soften. Strain and allow to cool.
2.  Using the small-size holes of a box grater, grate the carrots into a pot and add the sugar.
3.  Cook over moderate heat while continually stirring until all their juices are evaporated and softened and a paste-like consistency.
4.  Stir in the hazelnuts and cinnamon and mix thoroughly to combine. Use a spoon to blend until you create a thick paste.
5.  Cook for an additional 1-2 minutes before removing them from the heat.
6.  Sprinkle coconut flakes into a rectangular fridge-safe dish.
7.  Pour the carrot mixture over the coconut flakes and spread the mixture evenly.
8.  Scatter the remaining coconut flakes over the top and allow to cool at room temperature before transferring to the refrigerator.
9.  When the dessert is cooled, slice and dip into the coconut flakes.
10. Enjoy.

# Turkish Delight

This Middle-Eastern sweet treat needs no introduction. Suffice to say, no store-bought version of Turkish Delight will even come close to this homemade recipe.

**Servings:** 32

**Total Time:** 1hour 30mins

**Ingredients:**

- Nonstick cooking spray
- 4 cups granulated sugar
- 2 tsp freshly squeezed lemon juice
- 4½ cups water (divided)
- 1¼ cups cornstarch
- 1 tsp cream of tartar
- 1½ tbsp rosewater
- 2-3 drops of pink food coloring
- 1 cup confectioner's sugar

**Directions:**

1. Line a 9" square baking pan with foil and spritz the foil with nonstick cooking spray. Put to one side.
2. Add the sugar, fresh lemon juice, and 1½ cups of water in a pan over moderate heat.
3. Stir until the sugar entirely dissolves and bring to boil.
4. Brush the sides of the baking pan down with a damp pastry brush to prevent any sugar crystals from forming. Fit a candy thermometer on the pan.

5. Continue to boil the mixture and without stirring until the mixture registers a temperature of 240 degrees F.

6. When the syrup is approximately 225 degrees F., prepare the remaining ingredients.

7. Add the remaining 3 cups of water to a second, larger saucepan, and add the cornstarch along with the cream of tartar, whisking until the starch entirely dissolves and is lump-free.

8. Put the saucepan over moderate heat and bring to boil, while whisking continually until the mixture forms a thick paste.

9. When the syrup reaches 240 degrees, remove the pan from the heat. Pour the syrup into the cornstarch mixture, whisking until entirely combined.

10. Turn down to low heat and simmer, while whisking every 8-10 minutes or so, for approximately 60 minutes in total, until the candy is thick, glue-like, and a pale golden-yellow color.

11. When 60 minutes have elapsed, remove the pan from the heat and stir in a few drops of pink food coloring until you have achieved your preferred shade of pink. Next, stir in the rose water.

12. Pour the candy mixture into the prepared baking pan and set aside, uncovered, overnight.

13. The following day, take the candy out of the pan using the aluminum foil as handles.

14. Lightly dust a clean work surface with the confectioner's sugar. Flip the candy out onto the sugar.

15. Take the foil off the back and lightly dust the surface with sugar.

16. Using an oiled knife, cut the Turkish Delight into an evenly-sized square.

17. Dust both sides of the squares with confectioner's sugar; this will prevent them from sticking to one another.

18. Serve and enjoy.

# Valencian Orange Cake

This traditional Valencian cheesecake-style cake is bursting with a bold citrusy flavor. Perfect for serving alongside a hot cup of afternoon tea or mid-morning coffee.

**Servings:** 8

**Total Time:** 4hours 30mins

**Ingredients:**

- Butter (to grease)
- 6 ounces digestive biscuits (crushed into crumbs)
- 2 ounces butter (melted)
- 25 ounces cream cheese
- 2 ounces granulated sugar
- 3 ounces fresh-squeezed orange juice
- 10 ounces mandarin segments

**Directions:**

1. Grease a 9" springform cake tin with butter.
2. In a bowl, combine the crushed biscuits with the melted butter. Press the mixture into the base of the cake tin and chill for 15 minutes.
3. In the meantime, beat together the cream cheese, granulates sugar, and fresh orange juice until smooth and combined.
4. Pour this mixture over the base and chill for 4 more hours.
5. Decorate the cake with fresh mandarin segments before serving.

# Zabaglione

Impress your family and friends with this classic Italian dessert made with sugar, egg yolks, and sweet Marsala wine.

**Servings:** 6

**Total Time:** 45mins

**Ingredients:**

- 6 egg yolks
- ⅓ cup sugar
- 1 tsp grated lemon peel
- Pinch ground cinnamon
- 2-3 drops vanilla essence
- ¾ cup sweet Marsala wine
- 1 cup heavy cream, whipped
- Biscotti (to serve)

**Directions:**

1. Add the egg yolks and sugar to a stainless steel bowl.

2. Add the grated lemon peel along with the cinnamon and vanilla essence.

3. Pour in the wine.

4. Fill a pan, half full of water, and bring to simmer before reducing to low heat.

5. Place the bowl containing the custard over the water while making sure that the bowl's bottom does not come into contact with the water.

6. Whisk the custard mixture while making sure that the water does not come to a boil. It is important to whisk as this traps the air in the egg yolks and helps to create a fluffy and light mixture.

7. Continue to whisk until the mixture's volume triples, is frothy and pale. Once it reaches the desired consistency, remove the container of custard from the pot. Continue to whisk to avoid the sauce sticking to the container. Allow to cool a little.

8. Whisk the heavy cream until it can hold a soft peak. Add the whipped cream to the cool custard and with a metal whisk, gently fold them into one another*.

9. Spoon the zabaglione into individual dessert dishes and serve with biscotti.

*Serve the zabaglione warm or cooled. To serve cool, put to one side for approximately 15 minutes before folding in the whipped cream.

# Zuppa Inglese

Zuppa Inglese, or English soup, is a creamy Italian dessert that has its roots in the English trifle.

**Servings:** 8

**Total Time:** 9hours 35mins

**Ingredients:**

**Custard:**

- 2 cups whole milk
- 1¾ cups sugar (divided)
- 4 tsp cornstarch
- Pinch of kosher salt
- 3 large-size eggs
- ⅓ cup candied orange peel (diced)
- 2 ounces bittersweet chocolate (finely chopped)
- 3 cups water
- ¼ cup rum
- 2 cups heavy cream (chilled)
- ⅛ tsp ground cinnamon
- 36 ladyfinger sponge biscuits

**Directions:**

1. Add the milk to a pan and place over low heat.
2. Whisk in ½ cup of sugar followed by the cornstarch, and a pinch of kosher salt, and bring to simmer to dissolve the sugar.

3. In a bowl, whisk the eggs. While you whisk, slowly pour the hot milk into the eggs to temper. Return the mixture to the pan and set on moderate-low heat, and cook while whisking and stirring, until the mixture just simmers and begins to thicken.

4. Remove from the heat and scrape into a bowl to cool.

5. Stir in the orange peel and chocolate. Transfer to the fridge for a minimum of 60 minutes, until thickened and chilled.

6. For the syrup: In a pan, bring 3 cups of water and 1 cup of sugar to boil. Boil until the syrup is reduced by 25 percent. Remove the pan from the heat, stir in the rum, and allow to completely cool.

7. To assemble: Whip the cream along with the remaining ¼ cup sugar to create soft peaks. Fold approximately half of the whipped cream together with the cinnamon into the now chilled pastry cream.

8. Make a flat layer with approximately half of the ladyfinger sponge biscuits and brush with the syrup.

9. Spread the remaining pastry cream over the top in an even layer before spreading with the whipped cream.

10. Crumble the remaining ladyfinger sponge biscuits over the top and chill in the fridge overnight.

# Author's Afterthoughts

*thank you*

I would like to express my deepest thanks to you, the reader, for making this investment in one my books. I cherish the thought of bringing the love of cooking into your home.

With so much choice out there, I am grateful you decided to Purch this book and read it from beginning to end.

Please let me know by submitting an Amazon review if you enjoyed this book and found it contained valuable information to help you in your culinary endeavors. Please take a few minutes to express your opinion freely and honestly. This will help others make an informed decision on purchasing and provide me with valuable feedback.

*Thank you for taking the time to review!*

*Christina Tosch*

# About the Author

Christina Tosch is a successful chef and renowned cookbook author from Long Grove, Illinois. She majored in Liberal Arts at Trinity International University and decided to pursue her passion of cooking when she applied to the world renowned Le Cordon Bleu culinary school in Paris, France. The school was lucky to recognize the immense talent of this chef and she excelled in her courses, particularly Haute Cuisine. This skill was recognized and rewarded by several highly regarded Chicago restaurants, where she was offered the prestigious position of head chef.

Christina and her family live in a spacious home in the Chicago area and she loves to grow her own vegetables and herbs in the garden she lovingly cultivates on her sprawling estate. Her and her husband have two beautiful children, 3 cats, 2 dogs and a parakeet they call Jasper. When Christina is not hard at work creating beautiful meals for Chicago's elite, she is hard at work writing engaging e-books of which she has sold over 1500.

Make sure to keep an eye out for her latest books that offer helpful tips, clear instructions and witty anecdotes that will bring a smile to your face as you read!

www.ingramcontent.com/pod-product-compliance
Lightning Source LLC
Chambersburg PA
CBHW022155150726
47992CB00002B/796